Frayed

Frayed

Poetry and Thoughts from an Unraveling Mind

David A. Gibbons

David Gibbons

2018

First Printing
October 2018

Cover Design
Jacob Steininger
Star 7 Creative
star7.myportfolio.com

ISBN: 978-0-692-04300-4

Published By
David Anthony Gibbons
caged.in.ink@gmail.com
www.cagedinink.com

Ordering Information:

Special discounts are available on quantity purchases by corporations,
associations, educators, and others. For details, contact the publisher at
the above listed email address.

For the phantom in my head: without you my pen would be dry.

Table of Contents

I would like to give a special thanks to Jackie Cordova, Wacey Connor, and Alex Akins for fixing my terrible grammar. Thank you all for being willing to sift through the mire of mistakes that was my first draft.

Thank you Wacey for being my brother in life.

Thank you Alex for having such a kind heart.

Thank you Jackie for choosing to love me.

Preface

I have come to terms with myself. In loud places full of smoke and broken memories, and in a screen lit room filled with the clicks of a mechanical keyboard. My life has been no different than yours. There are no miraculous examples of downtrodden luck, nor impressive feats of universal punishment or pain. I simply experienced heartbreak. For me the brokenness of my heart spread throughout my body like a disease, until it finally reached my mind. My reality had been built upon the foundations of love, and when it was taken, my reality began to crumble. In my life, nothing has grabbed my attention more than love. Careers never ruled my mind, nor did money. Never has the longing for a large estate or fancy cars crossed my mind. Measuring my life by my advances in my career, or by the amount of good I do in this world never amused me. I only valued love. I built my world view upon it, and measured my worth by it. The extensions of me: my joy, optimism, spirituality, dedication, and personal motivation were all rooted in my concept of love.

Love was my sense of purpose, and my answer to the question "Why am I here?" In my euphoric state I gladly allowed my foundation to shield out the truth of reality. I willingly believed time could not affect me, believed wholeheartedly the world wanted good things for me. My love could never fade. My personality would never falter. Drugs and alcohol would never play a part in my life. I knew the world was full of evil, it had been since the dawn of time, but I believed the pain was not meant for me. My naivety made me vulnerable. My concept of love was flawed, as was how I determined its success. I put my faith in others, examining love under a microscope.

While love was my foundation, the recipient of my love became my cornerstone. I had no hopes nor desires outside of her. I used to always tell her this. She would ask where I wanted to live, where I saw myself in ten years, what my dreams were. My answer was always, "with you." In our youth, it seemed a simple display of affection. A claim, or maybe affirmation, that nothing in the world mattered besides her. For me; however, this was not adoration or hollow praise. For me, the answers held true. I had built my life on the concept of love, and placed my faith in the one whom I loved. Nothing else mattered.

The love I had for her was my cornerstone, but what created the foundation of my being was the example of love found between my parents. The two instances happened almost simultaneously, the removal of my cornerstone was quickly followed by the separation and divorce of my parents, which eventually resulted in my foundation crumbling entirely.

I know now, looking back, I romanticized their relationship. I placed upon them the burden of being symbols, essentially removing their humanity. Humans fail constantly, but I had rid them of their ability to fail. To me it had seemed they had overcome so much adversity. They had conquered the tribulations of life and made it to the serene valley on the other side. Perhaps this is a testament to their quality and caliber as parents. I lived with them for eighteen years and never once saw a glimpse of instability, but life is cruel. The trials, that in my mind they had conquered, had each taken their toll. Years of pain had built, love faded, and life continued.

While years of life slowly ebbed and flowed, and occasionally crashed and stole, the marriage of my parents began to falter. After twenty two years, the marriage ended. The weight of pain felt by my mother, father, and sister was immense. The example with which I forged my values and beliefs had failed, while the extension of my values and beliefs, the one I loved, left me. It created a stew of pain and confusion and loss.

I had to deal with my broken heart, but also the slowly dawning dread of realizing my place in reality was fading. I no longer knew what I wanted. I began to experience a multitude of feelings, fleeting twinges of thought that would never completely leave my mind. Mixed with the typical feelings of heart ache and loneliness were the resounding traits of anxiety, disassociation, forsakenness, emptiness, loss of purpose, and loss of hope. At the time, and to this day, I have difficulty describing the emotions I feel. They are never one simple, describable thing, but instead deep, complex canyons of thought and feeling.

Through various stages I began to fall, and as I did I felt myself begin to unravel. I became numb. With the quick loss of my foundation I struggled to find a reason for simple things in life. Everything had once pointed to her, but when she left, nothing pointed anywhere. Everything seemed distant and unattached. I felt the need to write. So I did.

Soon, I came to the conclusion that suffering is not simply about making it through the pain. Suffering is much more complex, and is different for everyone. For me, it was about sitting amongst the hurt, feeling and examining everything. These poems saved me. They were my life line to a new reality, and they reshaped me. They helped me cage the demons that plagued my soul and seal my thoughts in ink, thus giving me the opportunity to continue living a life worth living. I published so that you might find a little peace as well. If not in the words, then maybe in the simple fact that you are not alone.

Free Write September 30, 2015

The ruin of the storm tears and claws at the ragged ship. Waves flash from the depths of the deep, flinging themselves against the bulging wood. They lash out with malice at the vessel that refuses to sink. Her brothers and sisters litter the floor. Ghosts of hope longing to feel another join them. Another victim of pompous belief in the course set forth. Too prideful to turn back, too humble to push on.

Consumed

My fire lived. A small flick of heat created an ember. With gentle coaxing and care the ember grew bold. Sure of itself, the ember burst forth into the ink of Night. The blaze reached for the moon; begging to grow higher, grow brighter. A child reaching for his mother, the only resemblance of himself. As my fire was stretching to reach the eternal light, the permanence of the moon, the black of Night struck back. Quickly creeping in with his sister Cold. The two jealous siblings of deceit lay upon my blaze. Spoiling the pure, bright glow. Destroying the hopeful light. Obliterating the dream of eternity, because they were ashamed of themselves. They lashed out at what they did not know, killing the beauty that startled them. My blaze fought back. Pushing with the entirety of himself. The desire to be with the moon filling him, and hurting him. The realization that the evil would soon win. The realization that he would lose and be choked, with only the knowledge of losing the moon surrounding him. My fire died. The ghost of desire filled the voided space. Night and Cold danced and cherished the perished beauty. The ghost of my fire spread and built. The hopelessness, anguish and loss filled the space and drifted towards me. I let the ghost surround me, enter me, consume me. My fire lived. My fire died.

How

How do I begin to encompass
the complexities of my heart?
The sheer pain of my soul?
A tooth sunk deep to my core,
who makes her presence known
with every beat
and subtle course of blood.
The unending heat
of a drowning soul.

Friends

Move on!

Wait!

Be free!

Hope!

How?

I can't,

even,

breathe.

The Beach

I walk along a strip of sand nestled by the water.

Where an expanse of future stretches before me,

and the past reaches far behind my heels.

When I look back I see the beauty of a sunset,

glistening off two sets of footprints in the ground.

When I look ahead I see a storm taunting me,

slowly bubbling up ready to strip away the sand.

Yet I still watch the ground and examine every grain,

hopefully awaiting the prints of You to return.

As I walk the water pushes foam against my feet,

just to remind me the past is being washed away.

So I stop after every step to turn and look back,

back at the footsteps slowly being taken by the sea.

The Sonnet of Unrequited Love

I wear a silver ring around my neck.
It anchors me to memories and hope,
holding me to peace on life's dreaded trek,
a brazen shield to hate, with which I cope.
My ring will see the seasons shift and fade,
the rise of suns and end of many days.
My ring will see my very life cascade
through joy, but mostly into painful haze.
Every day I drape my silver burden
across my chest, and let hope fill my soul.
Hope that frees me, then makes the void harden,
but sends memory to take her dark toll.
It keeps me in desire, stuck in the past
until my silver ring is hers at last.

Words

       Goodbye.
I play with words daily.
Mold them, shape them,
raise them and release them.
Words are my strength,
the power of my
pen and of my tongue.
When she said Goodbye
my friendship with words
was destroyed.
That one word erased
all others, consuming life
it pressed through my soul.
Tore it, tainted it.
The word held memory, but
mostly an empty future.
It was a soft word,
choked out through tears.
I was broken and ruined
when she said
       Goodbye.

November 30

Today is our anniversary.
You would be here.
>   But you are gone.
We would embrace after absence.
Discuss the little things,
and I would breathe in your hair.
>   But there is only
>   pain.
I would have held you tight,
tied my fingers to yours,
and embraced the night.
>   But instead I am
>   alone.
You would have peered at me
as we walked, and felt comfort
before whispering your love.
>   But I only hear
>   despair.
I would have shown you rings.
Examined each one through
the haze of love and rising future.
>   But now I am
>   hopeless.
We would pull each other in,
as I take each hand and kiss
it once, before kissing you.
>   But I am
>   empty.
You are not here.
Today was our anniversary.

Rules

You left me 55 days ago.

Poetry has many rules.

Some are written down,

but most are understood.

This poem is breaking one.

       You are not to use a relative time when writing a poem.

But this poem is like me.

As time moves and changes.

This poem and I will be stuck.

Sealed to this hour and day.

Forever 55 days since you left.

Tyrant

I awoke from the cold sweat.
The grip of tangled emotions
that were coursing veins of Fear,
Hate, Bitterness and Loneliness
coiled tightly around my soul.
They created a terror of illusion.
Made a façade of the world.
Every color and face swirled
together in a complete fog
of anguish, grief and sorrow.
I walked surrounded by emotion.
Hate quickly raced behind me.
Bitterness and Loneliness took
me arm in arm, and held me tight.
In front strode Fear.
Nothing was real.
Nothing was fake.
Everything was pain.
My mind attacked the wretchedness
driving my companions away.
When they left, the grip on my soul
did not loosen, but shattered,

leaving a void where once I felt.

The dream of your loss has passed,

leaving only the reality of your loss.

Colors are clear but have been tainted.

Faces smile, but I cannot see yours.

The emotions that haunted me fled,

but in their stead a new king rose,

the unyielding ruler that is Despair.

He does not guide me nor taunt me.

He simply fills the void within my soul.

I Hate the Night

I am awake.

I will not sleep.

You chased me from my dreams.

Each night I visit you in painful memory.

Each night I awake, to painful reality.

I hate the Dark.

I hate the clock and every stroke of time.

Each day I suppress the pain.

Each day I slowly build a wall.

Brick by brick I shield you off.

I shield you from my soul and mind.

Each night the wall crumbles.

The essence of you pours into my soul.

It fills my mind with your stillness.

It fills my mind with your beauty.

I hate the night.

I am awake.

The Muses of Old

Calliope can help me write
the poetry of my life.
Clio can help me recall
the tales of bards.
Euterpe can help me sing
my many lamentations.
Erato can help me scribble
the songs of my heart.
Melpomene can help me tell
the sorrows of my soul.
Polyhymnia can help me lift
my pain to heaven.
Terpsichore can help me dance
for the small joys of life.
Thalia can help me laugh
at all my past mistakes.
Urania can help me look
to the stars for hope.
Only you can return my love.
The only muse I need is you.

Tracks

I went back to the tracks.
Yes the tracks where I wrote of freedom.
The place where I experienced liberation,
in water falling from my underwear.

I went back to the tracks.
Stretched across that hazel water.
Full of warm summer night memories,
and the buzz of things once started.

I went back to the tracks.
Where I first kissed your lips.
The coal train rumbled past our embrace,
forced us closer, and coyly tossed your hair.

I went back to the tracks.
The linchpin that bound my love to earth.
Where darkness shielded our subtle kiss,
and made my soul boldly reveal itself.

I went back to the tracks.

I went back to your memory.

I went back to our playful start,

just to feel the Pain.

What will Heaven Hold

If I die, will heaven be my past?

I think so.

The spirit of your memory haunts my future.

She never leaves.

She walks in front radiating our time.

Every second together.

Each step she whispers to my soul.

Reminder of absence.

A drive filled with your voice and passion.

Where it started.

A summer night kiss on a bridge.

The very first.

A date to see the glow of Christmas.

Closeness of cold.

It shows me what my future could be.

What I want.

It is what keeps me moving forward.

My waking source.

If I die, it would surely follow.

The New Year

I became a part of the push
of happy faces mixed and swirled.
Another groove in a tree.
This New Year's Eve I did a lot,
but I did not kiss you.
A new year tradition was snuffed out,
as the last firework shattered the sky.

Tom Petty and I

I lived in a Tom Petty song.
The wind rushed through my windows
drying the creek water from our skin.
I drove into the slowly setting sun,
like a true Hollywood cliché.
My blonde beauty by my side
wearing a frilled purple bikini:
and a coy smile.
CCR played an anthem to the day,
as my Z28 carried us to the future,
and I boldly invited it to come.

...

Four years after I first hit play
the song has ended,
and made way for silence.
The creek remains unstirred.
The sun sets quicker now.
I sold the car.

Ginsberg Stole My Soul

Allen howled at society.

The naked heroin addicts had no homes.

Alleys filled with burnt ashes and memories.

And something about cock and balls.

I want to howl.

Scream at the future and her taunts.

The exposing glare of an empty path.

Breathe in the rancid flesh of possibilities.

Shred each tendril of pain.

The snares that grip my soul.

Pull it from my chest to see the cracks.

Then poke each one and see what made it.

Claw and rip the love I thought I knew.

Rebuke it so it may never come again.

Sleep

I no longer fear the night.
The empty space where once you slept
has been overrun by my unconscious body.
Sleep comes each night.

I no longer fear the night.
The cold sweats, terrors, pain and tears
have left me in a voided silence of ink.
Sleep comes each night.

I no longer fear the night.
The pain has dulled and left behind
only the twitch of my dreaming eye.
Sleep comes each night.

I no longer fear the night.
Why can I sleep when it has evaded me
and left me to panic in the black for so long?
Sleep comes each night.

I no longer fear the night.
Why have the dreams of you given way
to vacant nights of consuming darkness?
Sleep comes each night.

I fear myself; I no longer fear the night.
Has my heart begun to harden? Has Time begun to
eat away at your memory to take my past?
I hate myself; sleep comes each night.

A New Emotion

Why did You leave me?
Five months of poetry have poured
from my soul and not once have I asked.
I loved you with the entirety of myself,
made you my only wish and promised
nothing but my eternal devotion.
I would have gone anywhere for you.
I would have been anyone for you.
I would have never stopped loving you.

Why did You leave me?
I loved you more every day, cultivated
a bond of love completely unbreakable.
It was not the world I should have feared.
The bond I built was to ward off the evils of life,
but could not withstand lost faith.
I gave you my soul.
I gave you my life.
I gave you my eternity.

Why did You leave me?
I am left in a limbic state of strife eternal.
I write poetry to fill your void.

What will I do if that void is filled?

What will I do if I cannot withstand time?

Am I less a man? Do I love you any less?

I would have waited until the sun set on my final day.

But time has gnawed our past. Time has numbed my pain.

Why did you make me wait? Why did you risk our love?

Why did you test my faith?

Why did you leave me?

You or you

This poem is not for You.

I am angry.

I know not how to express the complexities of my heart.

The sheer pain of my drowned soul.

A tooth tore through it.

I recorded my grief, my pain, my panic, my desolation

now it is time to record my anger.

I feel a heat rising within me, a heat that burns my soul

attempting to dry it out and rid it of my self pity.

It laps away at the pain flooded cracks you left,

but each blaze leaves a burn.

I fear for my soul.

I fear myself for burning away the pain.

I once dreamed of breathing in your hair,

now I am simply trying to breathe.

You left me. You had reasons that I blessed,

and we parted in mutual hope and love.

But it is hard to see Future when we have no Present.

Future once stood in front of me with hope.

she beckoned us to come, I sped forth

handing Past our memories and joy,

but maybe I gave her too much.

Future has left my presence without a path,

leaving Past to wield our memories as a whip.

An iron nine tail dripping with our love.

She drove me forward promising your return,

but how could she know?

She only knows what we had.

Now Time has come to take her place.

She attacked Past with malice that has left nothing

but scattered memories and the dull ache of lost love.

Now I am left with only myself.

Myself and my burning soul.

Why have you done this to me?

Why did you destroy my Future?

Why did you allow Time to take our Past?

I still love You.

But You has started to only become you.

I have capitalized your pronoun as one would a God,

in a weak poetic attempt to create meaning of my craft.

It is so hard to love when you are not here to love.

I have tried to love your memory,

but now I can only love your idea.

Each poem has been crafted and molded.

Each poem has been art my soul produced.

This poem is messy, as a crime of passion would be.

I tried to use a meter.

I tried to use a verse.

I even thought about a rhyme.

All I have is the stream of my conscious mind and repetition.

I am not blaming you for taking my poetry,

but I am blaming you for this one.

This poem is not for You.

This poem is for you, and my burning soul.

Untitled

I sit behind my house at night.
Call the skylark to be my eyes.
Mine don't work anymore.
The haze is too thick.
It seals me to my porch.

I send the lark to the valley.
Where tar mixes with the scent of rain.
Where trees grow tall for lazy birds.
The place I left the first piece of my soul.
The first time I tore it for a memory.

I left when you choked out goodbye.
My soul drowned, but was whole.
The drips of pain flooded it.
Then filled it completely.
Then ran down my face instead.

Time came and stole away the days.
My soul remained drenched.
I welcomed hate to scorch it dry.
The pain wouldn't leave; I had no choice.
I burned my soul, burned the pain, maybe too much.

Time came again, I didn't notice.

The burns I invited withered my soul.

They left no room for pain.

They left no room for anything.

Only the ache of raw blisters remained.

Numbness slowly overcame me.

I no longer felt, no longer longed.

The scorches did their job.

They healed my pain

Then they took my life.

The sharp pain of your image broke through.

It entered me, and pressed through the cracks.

The charred shell resisted and pulsed.

The image worked deeper tearing away the scars.

Then broke free into the vacant core.

The image carried three drops of pain.

They settled into the bottom of the pit.

Made the burns sting, but fade.

My soul wretched at the sensations of feeling.

The pain came back and brought my longing.

I returned to the valley.

I knew I didn't have long.

My soul would soon sear the healed scars.

I went to the bridge.

The lynchpin of love.

The pain had swelled there.

Time had filled it.

All the drops I denied were left there.

I feared to flood my soul again.

I wanted to leave, but couldn't.

I walked through the memories.

The flood began to rise.

I found the one I needed.

The flood began to push in.

I raced to the anchor of our love.

I tore my soul.

Ripped out the piece with the drops.

I placed it on the ground.

A drenched offering to the past.

Then fled from the rising water.

The Untold Story of the Hell Bound Train

The tarnished brass casing executed a ballet of treacherous paces and rolls across the rider's knuckles. He watched with an insidious hatred growing within his head. As the casing danced, spurred on by the nimble nudging of his fingers, the heat within him pressed against his eyes. It filled him completely and carried his thoughts deep into himself; carried his mind into the fire that burned within him. There, seated against an aging bolder, the wildly twisting casing spurred on the rider's hatred for himself, and underneath the scornful Nevada sky, the rider's thoughts threatened to consume him.

*

* *

When the moon ruled the sky, and the badlands of Nevada were filled with scavengers and creatures the sun had held at bay, the rider made camp in a small borrow at the base of a rock face. He dismounted, giving his horse a thankful pat, and went about gathering dessert wood and devil grass to coax a fire into the world. He sat softly chewing on some dried meat, chasing it with some ale from his last stop in civilization. He looked into the embers of the fire. Perhaps he looked too long, for he began to see a few phantoms. Visceral representations of guilt pressing heavily on his mind must have been given life by the fire at his feet. He watched them, amused at the power of his mind. They swam upwards with each tongue of fire, and shrieked with each pop of settling wood.

His heart began to beat more rapidly, not to the point of stress mind you; he prided himself in his ability to remain calm. His still eyes and hands in the face of death are what have forced his reaper to wait so long. Many a time he has come to the end. He has turned the final page of his story four times that he can remember. The first, when he was only seventeen, occurred when he decided to impress the schoolteacher's daughter by jumping in the bull pen of his father's ranch. Her cotton dress was speckled with blue flowers, and caught the wind in a way that made him need to prove himself to her, as if one daring act would seal his immortality in her eyes and the eyes of the universe, perhaps increasing the likelihood of some ethereal breeze removing the dress completely. The bull did not respond well to the slap it received on the rump. It turned with frightful speed and power, and would have gutted the rider if he had moved back a second later. The enraged beast planted its feet and rested its darting eyes on the face of his assailant. It kicked at the crusted earth with a broad hoof, and snorted its contempt. The young rider heard the girl in the dress shriek, saw the bull coil its muscles tightly, so he smiled coyly. He steadied his nerves and fixed his eyes on the beast's back left leg, knowing it would be the first to move. The bull moved, he moved; the reaper left, and the dress never fell.

Five years later, the reaper once again heard the last page turn on the rider's story. This time the end was carried in the chamber of a Peacemaker owned by a man whose rage was as strong as his desire to gamble. The rider was in a small town that only offered whiskey, cards and girls, and perhaps the occasional bounty. He had been preying on local drunks in a game of Hold'em, when the owner of the Peacemaker noticed something protruding from the rider's sleeve. The rider wasn't a good card player, but he was a good talker with nimble fingers. The rider surveyed his victims as he prepared to win another pot, but before he moved to deal out three more cards for the river, he noticed the man across from him flick his eyes to the rider's sleeve. Then, saw the steel settle behind the man's eyes, and saw his shoulders tighten.

The man with the Peacemaker didn't take well to cheats, and had killed a man for less. The rider saw the man's thirst for retribution flood his face. He knew the man would most likely try to kill him, and knew he had overstayed his welcome in the town anyway, he might as well move on. The rider said no words, gave no tells; he simply kicked back from the table, sending himself tipping to the ground, at the same time he pulled leather and pumped three shots into the gut of the man with the Peacemaker before he could even draw. The rider rolled out of the fall, stood, then finished his whiskey and grabbed his winnings from the felt. He slowly walked out of the bar, mounted his horse and rode out of town, knowing he had added another chapter to his life.

Not two years after, the rider met his end once more in a frightful storm that slammed into the valley he was camped. The water rose and rose, and the rider ran and ran, then swam and swam. Three hours later he was clinging to a log caught in the flood. Waiting for the right time to release his grip and paddle for higher ground. The reaper watched all the events, this time a little less hopeful, for he now knew the rider, and knew he wasn't like most. The rider knew death could only come for him if he lost his focus. If he lost his ability to stay calm, if he began to fear death, then death would surely come. So the rider clung to the log for two more hours, never once fearing the rushing water. He ended up thirty-eight miles south of his camp. He had to walk west for sixty-two more miles to get to a town where he could steal a new horse and be on his way. As he rode, he gave a chuckle at the thought of besting nature itself.

The final instance the reaper came for the rider, was only two days ago. A small town sat on the hardpan of the Nevada badlands, only two days east of the rider's current camp. The town was small, but sat triumphantly upon the barren ground. For years it had sustained itself by slowly draining the life of a nearby copper mine. The rider had caught wind of the town's stature, and its life supply, and decided he might stop by. The mine rested five miles north of the town, just down Ashburry lane. While the mine held an abundance of copper, it required work, time, and a permit to take, and the rider was not fond of any of those qualities. Ashburry began at the southern point of the town's limits, and ran past the mercantile, barber, tanner, smither, crossed Spoke St, then ran right by the local bank. The people in town were not very rich, they lived modest lives, but they survived off the stores of copper in the back of the bank. Copper that was already taken from the rock, sitting in store rooms, and only required a gun to take.

The town sold the copper to Hansle and Co. for crops, meat, and other goods at the first of each month. The rider decided he would arrive at the town around the 30th, just to make sure the bank was brimming. He rode in, stopped at the mercantile for a drink, and cheated a few men in cards. When the sun grew heavy in the west he walked out, and made his way down Ashburry. He never was one to weave a plan; he found decisive action and hot lead typical got the job done, but he had never robbed a bank, and he figured such an occasion called for a plan. As he approached the bank he noticed an older couple hitching their horse and wagon to the post outside the blacksmith's shoppe. He sat for a moment and gave a grin to the serendipity he had just stumbled upon. A wagon could carry much more copper than a single horse, and the horse he rode in on was stolen anyway, seemed like a good time to get another.

He pulled down the brim of his hat, and stepped into the bank. It was quiet. Only two women sat at the counter, one looked up and smiled at the stranger. He wasn't feeling particularly talkative so he got right to business. He drew both pistols and pointed them at the women, and asked them if they wouldn't mind joining him in the lobby, and they obliged with muffled shrieks and quick steps. He kept one gun trained on the women, and took a lantern off the wall to the left of the counter. He smashed it on a stool, then poured the oil onto the floor of the lobby. He grabbed another lantern from the other wall, and lit it with a match from his tobacco pouch. The flame grew strong, and the rider handed it to one of the ladies. Then he asked the other woman to fetch a rope and tie the woman up. He waited in the stillness of the lobby, thinking which city would have the best price for his copper. The woman returned and obediently tied the woman holding the lantern. Her legs and arms were bound and the lantern rested neatly in her hands.

The rider then asked the unbound woman to kindly help him with the copper in the back. She hesitated, but started moving when he raised his pistol once more. They loaded the copper into two burlap sacks, filling them until they were each around fifty pounds. With the sacks in tow he made his way to the exit. He positioned the bound woman near the door, she was sobbing at this point, and he positioned the other woman in front of him. Before he walked out, he told the woman in front to walk to the wagon across the street, if she screamed or ran he would kill her. If she tried to fight he would kill her. If she walked quietly to the wagon and carried one of the sacks, she would live.

With one quick check of his surroundings he holstered his weapon, and walked out the door. He and the teller made three trips to the wagon before anyone noticed what was going on. On the fourth and finale trip, things took a turn. As he placed the last two bags in the wagon, the owners of the wagon returned. They obviously didn't take kindly to their wagon being commandeered and then it appeared they noticed the fear in the teller's eyes, because the man who owned the wagon looked at the woman, then at the bags, then at the bank, but before he could look at the rider, he was dead. The rider had drawn and put a bullet between the man's eyes. He grabbed the now shrieking woman, placed the barrel of his gun against her temple, and moved into the middle of Ashburry lane, and waited. He waited as the crowd grew. He waited as guns were drawn. He waited until the sheriff stepped through the crowd and looked at the scene the rider had created.

The rider did not move, simply stated the obvious; he would kill the woman if anyone made a move towards him. The crowd looked around, and the rider kindly asked them to lower their weapons; unless they thought 400 pounds of copper was what her life was worth. When the weapons lowered he shuffled back to the wagon. He placed the terrified woman on the horse, then mounted behind her. With a slight kick the horse moved forward, and the crowd began to part. Through all this, the reaper watched the rider, thinking he had finally made a mistake. The people in this town would surely kill him. If they do not shoot him now, they would catch him eventually and hang him by the neck. The rider knew this too, and wasn't keen on dying just yet. He moved his pistol from the temple of the woman, and pointed it back at the bank. Pointed it at the entrance where the bound woman still stood sobbing, holding the lantern. No one had noticed her among the spectacle in the street, and a fire was sure to stall the sheriff for quite a while.

A quick squeeze of his index finger was all it took. All it took to extinguish the life of the woman in the bank. All it took to send the lantern falling from her now slack hands. All it took to engulf the bank in flames. A single squeeze was all it took to end a life, and end the livelihood of an entire town.

He kicked his new horse forward, westward, and out of town. The woman trembled in front of him. The town screamed and cried behind him. An itch began to form within his mind. He wasn't sure what it was, it was a small pull within him; an unreachable sensation, similar to the feeling of a coming sickness.

The moment when you first feel the crawl of fever across your skin, unsure if it was a chill from the wind, or something more malevolent. The rider pushed the feeling out with thoughts of the coming cards, whiskey and women he could buy with the money from the copper. The unwilling pair rode about three miles west before the rider stopped the horse. He dismounted, and pulled the woman off. She began to shriek and shake violently, and inevitably urine began to run down her leg. The rider told her to be calm, told her, her people would be coming to fetch her soon. He told her to tell the sheriff and his posse to return to the town, tend to the dead, and start rebuilding the bank. If they decided to seek retribution, they would only find desolation, and a bullet in the gut for each of them. The woman quickly nodded her head in compliance. He looked at her for a moment, weighing her fear and honesty, then left her in the wasteland.

One hour later the sheriff and his men approached the woman. The rider could see from his vantage point on a near-by butte they were armed to the teeth. They rode seventeen strong. He watched the sheriff dismount and embrace the woman. They exchanged words as the woman mounted the horse of a man in the back of the party. The sheriff stood, staring into the west; perhaps trying to see the rider, perhaps simply looking for an answer. He lowered his head, kicked a plume of dirt, then remounted and lead the party back into town. The rider lingered, watching the party ride away. When he was satisfied he made his way down the butte, and decided to make camp near a sheer rock face that could block the wind and block his fire from the sight of the town. As he built the fire, he felt the itch return, but he ignored it as he sparked flames on dried grass. He sat near the small flame and watched it grow.

By the time the fire was fully grown, the itch in his head had grown and spread as well. His thoughts raced as his heart struggled to pump cooled blood to his trembling fingers. He wrung his hands in an attempt to stop the foreign sensation. The rider had never experienced guilt before. Perhaps all his deeds had been justified, by either him, or by nature; but this deed, the burning of the woman in the town, he could not justify. He had killed men before, but they were always drunken gamblers, or murderers. Each time he had tempted fate, his reason was so that he may live. Self-defense he thought, or in the case of the school teacher's daughter and the bull, desire. The rider had even bested nature itself, but only so he could live another day. The evil he had committed, the sins he poured into the earth, were always counteracted by equal sin, or self-preservation. How was killing the woman, burning her alive, self-preservation? She had not wronged him, she was simply a tool he had used to satisfy his greed. The rider looked towards the setting sun, and felt his heart falter. Quickly, he pushed the guilt down deep, and focused on the money he had made that day.

*

* *

Reapers handle the transfer of a soul from our reality to the next. They are the ferrymen who guide the way between the realms of Death and Life. Death had taken notice of the scene the rider had caused, and of the innocent blood he spilt. Death is constant, the untouchable balancer of the scales of time. Life comes, but it always must go. Humans were never designed to walk the earth for eternity, that right is reserved for higher beings, but when life is taken too soon, Death takes note. Most of the time, when a reaper brings him a soul too soon, the souls owner lived a desolate, disparaged life. They sinned until their humanity began to fade. Death welcomes those souls with glee, but some souls are pure and innocent. They may be tainted with subtle scars of drink and sex, but they still hold tight to their humanity. When one of these souls comes to Death, the scales tip. Life becomes diminished by the loss, and if too many innocents enter the realm of Death, life begins to falter.

He once explained the process to a poet who had sold his soul to understand the universe. Death explained to the poet that he and Life are siblings. They are the constants of the universe. She gives, and he takes. The budding leaves in spring, must be taken by him in Autumn. The bear cub will grow, then fade, and will be taken by him. The human child will eventually grow old, and slip into his embrace. The poet was revolted. He wanted a way to prolong his life, he wanted what men had searched their whole lives for, he wanted eternal life. Death chuckled. Then told the poet the realm of man was never meant to be everlasting. Without him, without Death, Life would have no meaning. If he did not take the leaves in Autumn, why should they bud in the spring? If the graying bear did not enter Death's realm, why should the bear be born? If the human never withers away, what purpose does the human have to live? Death paused. My sister gives each earthly being breath, but what value is that breath if it is never taken away. I am the one who has given meaning to the world in which you live. Without me, man would never have purpose. They would never innovate and create. They would never love and hate. They would simply breathe.

When men such as the rider take an innocent life, when they snuff out humanity simply because they can, the balance of reality is tilted. Humans are governed by higher beings. Through the millennia, men have worshiped many manifestations of these beings. Through rise and fall of civilizations, gods have come and gone. Death told the eager poet the truth; the truth about the reality on the other side of ours, but the poet never shared what he learned. Some think he was frightened by the truth, worried humanity would not accept the answer. Yet others believe the poet realized a constant of the relationship between gods and men; belief. Belief is a foundation of human life. Belief we may one day find love. Belief we will line our pockets with silver. Belief our mistakes do not dictate or futures. Belief in a world beside this fading one we reside in. If the answer to the validity of a god that rules over another realm were answered; true or false the result would be the same. Man would no longer need to believe in an afterlife, or lack thereof, and thus would slowly have no use for belief at all.

Death would no longer be a fleeting state of existence. Death would be the end. All of the goodness brought into the world by Death, the sense of purpose and constant drive to create, would evaporate if man new what lay beyond this world. If there is an afterlife, one that is pure and untainted by the sins of our ancestors, why should we struggle in this world? If there is nothing after we are laid to rest, then why should there be strife to begin with? If we are simply destined to turn back to dust, why fret over what you accomplish in the period between birth and death. Belief spurs on humanity. Belief in another world, and the freedom to choose what you believe in, gives mankind enough motivation to ignore the ever-approaching shadow of Death.

Death beckoned the rider's reaper, and sent him back to earth with a vision. The vision was carefully carried to the rider's camp, where the reaper watched from beyond human sight. The rider was gazing into the embers of his dying fire. The reaper approached, and rested the vision on the shoulders of the rider. Soon the rider was sent spiraling downwards, through existence and time he fell, and landed in the depths of belief:

Heat. Visceral heat scorched the riders face, and filled his nose with the hollowness of air seared sterile by flame. An awful groaning filled his ears. Mechanical pounding and churning mixed with chilling groans filled the space. The moans made him retch and sped his heart, they rang out incessantly, but never grew above a steady rumble. They sounded too tired and forsaken to become screams, the ones who produced the terrible sounds were void of hope. The groans were hollow yet full of anguish. The only reason the unseen beings groaned, was the unwillingness of their bodies to contain the pain they felt, as if by groaning they could free some pain from deep within them.

The smell of rotting, burning flesh attacked the rider's senses, and a flash of blinding light cast treacherous shadows around him. For a moment, he saw where the groans were originating. Bodies riddled the ground around him. Sunken faces gazed painfully up at him. Their bodies were all but gone, and what remained was drenched in scarlet blood. Some of the bodies were missing limbs, some were smoldering slowly, but they all moaned.

Slowly the mechanical sound began to grow, and the rider became aware that he was moving. Another flash came, and the rider realized he was in the car of a train. In the darkness, he tried to find the wall of the container, with one hand over his face; futilely attempting to ward away the onslaught of smells and sounds attacking his senses, and the other outstretched. His free hand found a smooth surface and he leaned against it, but quickly a smoldering hand reached out from the blackness. He swiped it away, but yet another lashed out for him. Soon he was being pulled downward, yanked to the floor with the still breathing corpses.

Over the moans and churning of the train he heard a laugh, it struck his ears sinisterly. The sound did not match the desolation around him. It was a strange noise compared to the bodies, the burning flesh, the anguished distorted men and women around him. The laugh rang out once more as he felt the train gain speed. The sounds grew louder. The bodies groaned deeper. The smell of burning flesh and sulfur burned his eyes and nose. The heat began to sear his skin.

His heart was pounding, it threatened to break through his ribs at any moment. The hands still clawed at him longingly, then one corps bit his shoulder, drawing blood. Another threw its mangled body on top of his. The rider's clothes were singed from his body, and he could smell his own flesh burning. Around him the bodies became more and more enraged at his presence. They began to lash out at him, tearing away his skin. They gnawed at his limbs, and gouged at his eyes. Amongst the throng of bodies, he even felt a sensation in his groin, and realized with creeping dread and remorse that he was being raped. The train gained speed, the heat continued to rise, and over the symphony of horror surrounding him, the laugh rang out once more. The rider could do nothing but weep.

Blackness met the rider when he awoke in a cold sweat. The sweat that comes when a fever is broken. His hands shook, his heart raced, and he realized his leg was warm and wet; he'd pissed himself. He brought his hands to his face and began to sob, a trembling sob like the woman he had held hostage not 4 hours earlier. After his tears ran out, and the piss began to dry, the rider looked into the embers of his fire. The guilt was overwhelming, and the visions and sensations of the burning train filled the recesses of his soul. He pulled out a spent casing from his pack, and set to work rolling it across his knuckles. The brass stilled his mind and hands, but sent him deep within himself.

He began to hate himself. It filled him completely now. The rider new the vision was what awaited him when death finally caught him. Was it hell? Was the laugh the laugh of Satan? Or was the train taking him to another place? It didn't matter. Where ever the train of wayward souls stopped, was not a place to spend eternity. He quivered once more, then quickly got to his feet, and walked into the wilderness. Darkness surrounded him, as dark thoughts filled his head. The rider had never feared before, but now he was terrified. What could he do to change the prophecy? What could he do to stay off the burning train?

Maybe a quiet life would be enough to make the devil forget about him. If he made camp in the desert, and never spoke to another sole; speaking only to God and killing only what he needed to eat, maybe he could die peacefully, and board a different train. Could he right his wrongs with good deeds? Could he turn his life around, or was it too late? Then a dark thought came to him as his handed wrapped around the butt of his pistol. Maybe he should end it now. He could prevent a life of worry, and punch his ticket right now, with the gun he held in his hand. Maybe the vision was a prophecy, and no matter how many good deeds he performed, his sins would always outweigh the righteousness.

The rider inhaled slowly, attempting to calm his nerves. He pushed away the suicidal thought. He had never run from danger before, never strayed from a challenge. Why take the easy way out now? If the vision was a prophecy, if he is destined to board the train, then the best thing he can do, is warn others before they punch their own ticket. His heart softened a bit at this thought.

Perhaps, absolution could be found in the saving of others. How many men would change their wicked ways if they too saw what he had seen? The rider walked back to camp. He pulled parchment from his saddle bag, and located a pencil he used to add his winnings from cards. He rustled the fire back to life, and sat himself next to it. He gazed at the blackness around him, sitting perfectly still, then allowed the demons to enter him. He filled his soul with the vision he had just escaped. The pencil hovered slightly over the paper, before writing four words at the top of the parchment:

"The Hell Bound Train"

The Witching Hour

Nothing is the same;

everything has changed.

My life isn't mine.

I am alienated from my body.

My soul has endured too much

it can no longer hold my spirit.

It drifts in the air above me;

limbic.

Time does not move.

The dullness has overcome existence.

The clock of my life is stuck

 on the witching hour.

Bleakness and obscurity shroud reality.

Possibilities exist;

I fear them.

Like the goblin crawling from the moor to feed.

The lycan distorting into a new body.

The ghoul searching for a soul to consume.

I feel them all.

Feel them rising

bubbling

coming.

I see the beauty of a woman,

but the lycan will have her soon.

I see the openness of friends,

but the goblins are upon them.

I see myself in the mirror,

but the wing beats of the ghoul reverberate.

> *Whom*

>> *Whom*

>>> *Whom*

There is nowhere to run

>> hide

>>> cry.

The witching hour never changes.

I cannot escape it.

> *Whom*

>> *Whom*

>>> *Whom*

There is no light in the distance.

Nothing to run to.

No one to run to.

> *Whom*

>> *Whom*

>>> *Whom*

Maybe I can fight.

I can rebuke the clock and force the hands to spin.

Force the hands of time to remove the vale.

      Whom

           Whom

                Whom

           Whom

      Whom

Or maybe I can die.

Reverie

I eternally swim through a reverie.
Viscously a bubble fills my head.
With a gurgle it consumes my body,
effervesces into my chest to cloud my soul.

The swarm of fizz surrounds my thoughts.
Cruelly it keeps me suspended in time.
My soul hangs softly in the world,
trapped in the reality of my musing.

Each drop of time is warded away.
Vacantly I feel my mind chase a ghost.
I am forever seated in the twilight of life,
desperately waiting for the sun to crest.

The Iceberg in My Cabinet

I read somewhere;
I do not remember where,
of an iceberg in a cupboard.

I enjoy the simplicity of it.
The unordinary, made mundane.
A cupboard, flat and still,
hiding what should not be.

I enjoy saying my life is the cupboard.
It is amusing to think about;
fun to question what my cabinet holds.

If I keep it closed, it is anything,
and everything, all at once.
Every path exists behind the door.
It holds my futures.

If I open the door, spread it wide.
The iceberg is revealed.
The path I am meant to take.

I do not like that.

I have gazed at that bleak path.

Watched it summon me.

Even took steps down it.

That path only carried pain,

and a feigning reality.

It wasn't the iceberg I wanted.

I think I will close the door.

Maybe I will glue it shut.

I will let the futures mix and settle,

and stride into life on my own.

Do you Know?

I loved you.

Do you know that?

I am not sure you do.

You do not like poetry.

Perhaps my words were lost.

I wrote a few ballads.

I wrote some sonnets.

I even wrote some rhymes.

They were for you.

I wanted to show you my love.

Wanted you to feel my soul.

Now they simply float.

They float like me.

You rebuked them, and me.

Now I have relics of my love.

I read them to see if my soul remembers.

See if it remembers how love felt.

Remembers the fullness of love.

They mostly slip through the cracks.

I try to stop them.

Try to hold them in.

Somehow they always fall out.

Blood from my slit wrist.

Do you know my pain?

I am not sure you do.

Vice

Maybe I could swim in alcohol.

That would surely numb the pain.

Maybe it would find my soul,

and drown it once more.

This time it could fill the cracks,

fight the memories that try to rest there.

Maybe I could use my body.

I could find new women.

I could flood my mind with beauty,

let it fill me with the dull spark of lust.

Maybe I could forget about my soul.

I could push it deeper with each new kiss.

Maybe I could dine on pills.

Let them free my mind.

Open my subconscious,

and let my thoughts drift.

Watch them float high above me,

far from the reality of my soul.

Maybe I could use my pen.

Write my pain on parchment.

Fill pages with every trial,

and capture each emotion.

I can rid the demons from my soul.

Cage them in the lines of ink.

Flowers in the Meadow

For Mom

We have no roots in life to hold us,

we toss and turn falling like debris.

I see you suspended in a meadow,

seated gently on a swing 'neath a tree.

I have watched the sun shine on you,

faintly warming your cheek.

You have sat upon your swing,

grazing flowers with your toes.

Now clouds have moved in quickly,

they covered up the sun.

Now the storm is upon you,

and only darkness it has brung.

Let the winds attack,

feel them claw and tear.

Let the clouds build above,

watch them boil and rage.

Smell the rain mixing with dirt,
hear the drops grow and spread.
Hold tight to the ropes,
that rise high above your head.

You cannot calm the storm,
the winds will not listen.
You cannot hide from the flood,
the rain sinks deep.

Let your legs dangle,
hovering softly o'er the dale.
The clouds will taunt and rage,
but you can sit amongst the gale,
and feel the flowers 'neath your feet.

Flowers in the Meadow: Cessation

For Mom

Sometimes the flowers wither,
crumble beneath your feet.
A quick frost moves in quietly,
settles between a single heartbeat.

The sun once shone upon you,
before the storm hid it away.
Now the frost has gripped the land,
quieting the swing to a humble sway.

Once your feet could dangle,
hover so softly o'er the dale.
Now the chill has forced you inward,
huddled against the tree so frail.

The flowers touched your toes,
as you listened to the raging gale.
The storm has passed and rains have dried,
only a brittle silence now prevails.

Winter has come to steal away the color,
cold fingers pry away each petal.
The ground has hardened in retribution,
life comes only in the form of a simple nettle.

The swing floats vacant in the air,
tossed by the occasional hollow breeze.
The sky has become stiff and void,
creating an aroma of unease.

You can hold yourself so tightly,
seated 'neath the silent tree.
You can rebuke the seasons for changing,
or you can rise up from your knees.

The Winter will not listen,
to your command she will give no heed.
Her grip upon the land will only flee,
when her sister Spring makes her concede.

Until that day grow bold,
go forth and gather seed.
Venture into the hollow land,
wherever the wind may lead.

Do not fall to your knees,

unless it is to dig a small hole.

A tiny preparation for the future,

where soon your seed can grow.

Walk forward into the stillness,

deep into the hardened world.

When the wind becomes to brisk,

do not stop and become furled.

Slowly lower yourself to the earth,

and reach into your pocket.

Place a single seed upon your palm,

and recite this simple sonnet:

Gather one seed, two seeds, then three seeds more,

as the winds whip and ground grows cold, press on;

into the uncanny wild you abhor.

Grow bold in knowing soon will come the dawn.

Do not repose from the chill brought wan,

but find your rest in the collection of a seed,

then add the token to your echelon,

pausing slightly to look out and take heed.

Notice the bleak land begging to be freed,

take satisfaction in your steady task.

Soon the south wind will come and be your lead,

your toil will end, in the sun you can bask.

Your boldness in the bleakness of winter will bear good fruit,

for now, in the renewal of Spring your seeds can take root.

False gods

The night has gathered.

Frost has sprinkled the window,

and darkness has filled the void,

forcing the world to pause.

I hold a woman against my chest.

Her brown hair swims across my body,

but all I see is silver blonde.

I want to love her.

I want to mix my life with hers,

but in the stillness of the night,

my past finds me once more.

I hear a quiet laugh resonate from the voided space.

Phantoms of the past illuminate the corners of my room.

You dance there, and softly speak.

I can never hear your voice, only a gentle laugh.

The visions swirl then coalesce.

An effervescent and fleeting beacon,

forcing my soul to shift, and pressing my mind to stir.

I sit

My mother has been dragged through heartache.

A pain I know too well,

Only her pain carries the weight of 22 years.

My pain only carried 4.

Time has reached the point where she begins taking.

Taking friends

Taking love

Taking life

I have no money to distract my idle mind.

I have refused the beckon of drugs,

and warded off the threats of alcohol.

So I sit.

I sit and watch the shadows creep across the ground,

and into my mind.

I feel the pain I have distracted with trivial comforts.

It sat quietly inside as I danced and laughed,

but now my feet are still.

My throat is shut.

I sit and let the pain creep into my veins.

Overdose

An intense feeling of deep affection.

Webster calmly defined the complexities of love.

Or is it the father forsaking his family?

Is it the son who wants to hate him?

Wants to fill his soul with rage,

rebuking the man he knew,

but fails, because the past reminds him of the park.

Reminds him of the tree in the corn field.

Makes him feel the countless lessons.

Is it the abandonment of connection?

The longing one feels for the one he lost.

The inability to have passion for another,

because someone stole away your soul.

Is it the crying mother?

Is it the addict son?

The distant daughter.

The insecure partner.

Is it the overwhelming desire to drown your soul,

if only to kill the flames of hate within?

Maybe it is the incessant reminder of a looming future.

The unyielding whips of a broken past.

The desolation of an empty present.

The Pickup

for father, and also for myself.

My feet warmed on the dirt caked floorboards as we jostled down the road. My father held the gaze of the horizon as his finger tapped against his thigh. His left hand was gripped tightly on the wheel; his thumb grazed over the tattered leather seams repeatedly. I turned away and engaged my mind with watching the rows of soybeans pass quickly by. A line of earth would present itself, straight as an arrow it would extend to meet the setting sun, then as it appeared, a flash of green would replace it with a new line of dirt. The steady pattern played with my eyes as they attempted to catch up with the racing rows. The heater ticked quietly and drowned out the words of the music playing softly. The notes coming from the radio created a haunting melody that demanded stillness. I was lulled into the infinite monotony of the passing crops and the wordless music that sat heavy in the cab of the truck.

We drove through the farmland with wordless love. The love that is felt; felt so heavily it becomes comfort. The truck came to rest on a worn piece of dirt on the rim of a field, just ahead rose a lone oak tree. My father unbuckled and shifted out of his seat and onto the ground. I quickly followed and we stepped towards the tree. Its branches reached outward trying to catch the wind. Its leaves rustled as the limbs danced with delight. The trunk held them tight as they frolicked in the setting sun. I ran my hand along its cinder bark, letting the grooves guide my fingers. As I walked, my attention drifted upwards to the ballet of life above me. Robins hopped from one dancing branch to the next and greeted each new limb with a soft chirp of gratitude. The leaves shifted back and forth, overlapping for a moment, before letting a pinhole of light slant through. My father sat back from the tree watching only me. His eyes gleamed as mine did, but for another reason entirely.

Without a word he stepped to me and handed me his pocketknife. I took it and etched my name in the side of the oak. The scar of my name permanently tied me to the massive tree. I stepped back to admire my work and felt my father's hand gently rest on my shoulder. He scuffed my hair and pivoted me towards the truck. We both looked at the pickup with admiration, then he said I should drive home. My heart leapt and my blood ran sparks throughout my body. Before I could answer we were walking towards it. He sat in the driver's seat and patted his leg. I clumsily climbed up and sat in his lap. He shut the door and turned the key. The truck moaned then came to life. As I gripped the wheel I was suddenly aware of the power I felt. The truck would obey me. Much as the wind conducted the mighty oak, I was the course setter for our journey home. My joy faded as fear quietly seeped into my body. As if my father felt my heart quicken, he pat my back and told me he had me, he told me we would be all right, and that he knew I could do it. I believed him. He slowly pushed the gas and I set the truck on course. The jostling increased as we ventured towards home. My joy overflowed and my heart was full.

We went faster and faster and my heart matched our pace. I held the wheel so tight my hands felt rooted to the truck. I took a turn and gained confidence, I felt invincible. I turned the wheel slightly as the road meandered to the left. Just as I began to straighten out we hit a rut in the dirt, the right side of the truck popped up and surprised me. We were going too far left, I quickly tried to reset our course but pointed the truck straight at the ditch on the right side. I had no time to think, only to worry. Just before we hit the ditch my father's arms reached around me and grabbed the wheel. He shifted the truck back center and away from the ditch. He slowed the truck to a halt in the middle of the road. I sat in his lap with the deep beating of my heart receding. Tears welled in my eyes. I failed. I felt defeated and scared. Then a subtle laugh caught my ears, and my father wrapped his arms around me. He picked me up and sat me in the passenger seat. I looked to him as he pat my leg. He said he was proud of me, he told me how great I had done. He looked at me with pure love and said I didn't need to be scared or worried, because he would always be there. He told me I would make mistakes, but he would always pick me up. He asked if I wanted to try again and I softly shook my head no. He moved the truck forward and headed home.

The sun set on the day, and rose on many others. Each day the boy grew and emulated his father. Many more drives occurred and life moved on. The boy made mistakes but his father always picked him up. When his course in life started to falter, his father was there to right it. Days came and went and the father watched the boy grow. He watched with joy and a heart of love. Every evening the sun would set on the dancing oak, but the name on the trunk remained. Storms came and threatened the tree. The sun beat down on it, and floods surrounded it, but still the name remained. Just as the scar on the tree never faltered, the fathers love never ceased to surround the boy.

Broken

The fog of you has surrounded my heart,

and forced me to break another.

I took her trust; I took her faith,

and I tainted it with my presence.

Another woman scorned,

because I can no longer love.

Another bridge crumbled,

because I cannot see my future.

Words

My words began our time together.

They sprang from my mouth and floated in the smoke.

They danced across the bottle tops,

before resting upon your ear.

Now my words have torn your soul.

They crept from my mouth bringing with them pain.

They scuttled through the air,

before sinking into your heart.

Crossroads

Last night I tried to sell my soul.
I walked to the crossroads,
the clichéd location of last resorts.
I slipped my hands into my pockets,
then meekly spoke the devil's name.

He sprang forth and spoke with words of ice.
His words were plain and direct,
carefully crafted from centuries of practice.
He held out a clean hand,
and asked what I truly desired.

I told him to take away my pain.
I told him I could not do it on my own,
nothing seemed to ebb the tide within me.
The devil grinned and softly inclined his head,
then quickly he snatched my soul.

He fled into the night clutching his prize.
I was left in the shameful light of the moon,
feeling the absence of pain within me.
I gazed blankly into the darkness,
enjoying the nothingness I had longed for.

As I left the hollow place,

the devil appeared before me,

and held out my soul.

He wore a grimace on his face.

He said he couldn't use it.

It had been sold to another.

Bound

I detest the rules that bind reality.
The ones that hold me to the earth.
They keep me from reaching you,
and seal me to the march of life.
I am bound to walk a path,
the same path we all share.
I stare at my feet as they toss up dirt,
and slowly carry me to death.

I detest the rules that turn the clock.
The ones that hold me from the past.
They force time to move through me,
and steal away the thoughts within my head.
I can never revisit blissful memories,
the ghosts of a happier time.
I can only move ahead,
and peer into the void.

Breath

I inhale a hollow breath as my soul cries out.

Desperate to feel its place in the universe.

The Phantom in my Head

An imposter haunts my sleeping mind.

She has donned your face and hair.

Every lock falls perfectly upon her shoulders.

She shows up when my feet sink into the earth.

When I visit foreign lands she follows me.

She is the only constant in the depths of my mind.

Her body matches the beauty of yours.

A coy smile brings a flood of memories.

On certain nights she gains mortality.

My mind descends below the witching hour.

On those nights, she even carries your scent.

For a year I awoke in a cold sweat.

I turned to your pillow, only to see it vacant.

For a year the phantom shadowed me.

She held me in a reality where I did not belong.

Each night she forced my mind to turn.

Each day I begged the sun to stay.

But now I see.

Her eyes are hollow and dull.

She must have forgotten to take them.

They do not pierce through me.

Vacancy resides where fierceness lived.

There is no glow of multitudes.

Last night I stared deep into them.

I searched the pools for a speck of you.

I found nothing but a void covered in blue.

In the Valley of the Khan

Last night I dreamed without my phantom.

I stared to long into the glassy pools of deceit,

now she has vanished from my imaginings.

I found myself on the edge of a dale,

the place Coleridge created with his pen.

A temple stood sheltered by decaying vines,

and the birds swooped a rushing stream.

Lush canopy sheltered my head,

while thistle clung to my feet.

I gazed at the world unfolding before me,

but only spied two ghosts among the trees.

King Kubla sat atop the temple,

lightly tossing pebbles down the steps.

Time has taken his lustful vigor,

leaving him senseless in a land of beauty.

The other ghost was that of Samuel,

dangling his legs in the rustling stream.

The loss of his mortality left him stranded,

bound as a wraith to his one true muse.

My ghost made no appearance in the valley,

not even a single strand of golden hair.

Perhaps she lost her hold upon me,

when I looked within her shallow eyes.

I wish my phantom would return to me,

return and fill the corners of my dreams.

While she forced binds around my waking soul,

she allowed my sleeping mind to wander.

Her presence stirred my body in the night,

as my mind remembered the sight of love.

Perhaps I gazed too deeply into her,

shattering the last piece I held of you.

Perhaps I am trapped in a foreign land,

with the ghosts of a poet and a king.

Flee

And what of the flutter in my chest?
The quiver of my fingertips?
The rattle deep within my bones?
My feet scratching at the dirt,
writhing at the mundane.
The fleeting of my eye,
and the dancing of my brain.
The ever-growing spark within me,
dripping into every vein.
I cannot find the lark,
the freer of my inner pain.
My ink has grown stale,
I only write lines I disdain.
My mind is sealed to my body,
trapped in a reverie chain.
If my mind is caged within me,
then my body must flee again.
I will listen for the deep bellow,
and leap aboard a passing train.
I will ease the binds of mind and body,
by venturing to a new terrain.

Retribution

I wish I could desire revenge,

but instead I desire you.

The leftover pieces of love ache,

retribution would be easier to hold.

I wish I wanted you to hurt,

by seeing me with another.

I heard a country song in passing,

it spoke of new bodies and new locations.

Flaunting a nubile woman,

to make the past squirm.

Filling myself with rage,

would be better than my current state.

Longing has dulled my senses,

and made me vulnerable.

Hating you would bring new life,

and permit me to move on.

Instead I feel desire, and wait.

Fabric I

i feel exposed
a loose stitch
in the fabric
of this reality

Fabric II

The world is loosely woven
Threads are stretched too thin
I feel myself nestled deeply
Between two frayed stitches
Maybe if I relax my mind
Let my body go cold and limp
I could slip between the webbing
Find a new world to reside in

Whirlpool on the Ceiling

The ceiling fan clicks in the night.

Agitated by years of spinning,

a bolt has loosened,

and now protests methodically.

The clicking pulls me deep into a trance,

sheltered by the darkness around me.

It gathers up the sounds of croaking frogs,

and restless floor boards within its blades.

It collects warm summer time breezes,

and gripping winter winds.

Words once spoken in the room,

small glances and grins,

all swirl into its grasp.

Every morning ritual and thought,

each peaceful slumber with you.

It pulls them all into a whirlpool,

hovering just above my head.

I feel them dripping on me,

each seeping deep within my mind.

The fan creaks once more,

then pours the memories towards me.

They spring downward and around,

enveloping my stagnant body.

Quickly they rush upon me,

and carry me to the past.

Out of Cowboy Exits III

I called Hollywood last night,

searching for a little peace.

They said they were out of sunsets,

and couldn't spare a happy ending.

Forced

If only my days were not tainted
by this phantom I have created.

If only I could walk with sure steps
and not question what will happen next.

If only I could once again return
to the youthful optimism I yearn.

If only holy matrimony grew boldly
from this lowly lonely testimony.

If only I could be with you like old times
instead of wasting my days forcing rhymes.

Power

Sleep is a free fall deep into another world.
A vast reality, bending to the will of my mind.
Yet it is hollow, for I always awake
to the dullness of this world,
where my mind has only one power,
the ability to alter a piece of paper.

Battle with a Tissue

My mother is selling the house.
The one with the barn and pond,
and the ghosts of both our pasts.
She didn't want to,
the ghosts held her mind.
They blew out the flame of possibility.
The walls bulged with their presence,
and each night they ventured into reality.
One night we battled the ghosts,
with iron, salt, and a box of Kleenex.

We rid them from the halls,
and chased them from the grounds.
They no longer held her mind,
and she could now move on.
The for sale sign is staked into the ground,
and freedom is on the horizon,
yet I feel a change within me,
as does my beautiful mother.
Perhaps amongst the fray of battle,
a few ghosts found new homes.

Metamorphosis

I was the one who made you smile,

and the one who calmed your nerves.

On long trips from home I soothed you,

and always pointed out the stars above.

My steps were light and full of life,

as I carried us both into the future.

Hearty optimism spilled from my veins,

mixing and coalescing within your heart.

I feared neither gods nor natural law,

but boldly taunted them with every thought.

Quickly I constructed an altar to your image,

seated it deep within the walls of my soul.

Doing so tore the seams that held my humanity,

but I filled them with positivity and hope.

Then you left and the altar crumbled,

and the wards within me began to falter.

I have felt the world try to break through,

each pain chipped into the vulnerable seams.

With no sight of you the hope began to fade,

then quickly my positivity fled.

My soul was left exposed and vacant,

holding only a crumbled throne.

To fight off the world I built new protectors,

doubt and despair became the shields within me.

Swiftly they brought anxiety to my once steady mind,

and swept bitterness throughout my bones.

I had replaced my humanity with an idol,

protected by wards that could not withstand time.

To save myself from the passage of reality,

I sheltered the hollowness with pain.

Shallow Grave

Life is not controlled by any laws.

She does what she wishes,

and to me she wishes pain.

Last night I dug a shallow grave.

It was only two feet deep.

I laid amongst the dirt,

and breathed in the musk.

My fingers toyed at broken roots,

while my eyes softly shut.

I wanted to see what the world looked like,

from the perspective of a dead man.

Did it slow at all?

Maybe hurt a little less?

Since I can find no peace within this world,

maybe solace would come to me in death.

Silence

Silence likes to nibble at my soul.

I hear the electronic buzz through the phone,

a symbol of my silent mother

letting slow tears trickle down her face.

Reality has gripped her tongue,

and now she can only cry.

22 years of love were torn apart.

Memories of a long reality ripped away,

leaving my mother in the midst of a cold one.

Death Waits in Dallas

Death does not wait for me in Samarra.

She is not waiting in the market streets,

and she has forsaken our agreed appointment.

She has taken it upon herself to find me now.

I hear her beckon with each thump of my feet.

Each stride forward carries heavy intentions,

and a frightful hollowness resounds within.

Once, the path my feet carried me on spread wide.

It wound its way through life,

taking time to open upon the dale,

forcing me to pause and enjoy the day,

allowing me to marvel at entropy unfolding.

Now, in your absence,

and perhaps the absence of myself,

the path has grown narrow,

and brambles have overtaken it.

It slopes ever downward,

forcing my strides to quicken,

and giving no dales to rest.

It extends to Death's outstretched hand.

I do not fear.

I simply resent the path.

I writhe at the incessant march,

and no longer marvel entropy.

The path has lost its subliminal nature,

and has simply become the tool that carries me further,

further from your embrace.

Do Over

I wish you could have met me now.
Eyes locking across a crowded room,
stale with smoke and shadowed faces.
My fleeting heart and last gulp of drink,
before making my way to you.
Slow dancing under the colored beams,
to the sounds of a slowly dying night.

Maybe we could write a better story.
I could drive you home while building courage,
strength to ask for your number.
O, what I would give to find that moment,
a dying night filled with the life of opportunity.
Ecstasy of possibility in the ending of the dark,
the hopeful goodbye of new love.

I would trade all the memories within me.
Rid the homeroom glances from my head,
and abandon the late-night drives.
Toss aside your voice on the phone,
throw out each softly spoken 'I love you'
Leave the image of silver curls behind,
destroying the symbolism in my mind.

I would even forsake the bridge.

Extinguish the incessant roar of the midnight train,

forget the smell of tar carried by a summer breeze.

Obliterate the sounds of the enveloping night,

and leave behind each glowing grin.

Reject the phantom memory of your touch,

free myself from the moonlit kiss.

Maybe I could sell them all.

Relinquish my memories to the highest bidder,

Time, Death, Past, they would all accept with glee.

I am not a better man,

I am worse now.

Time has aged my soul,

forced me to know myself.

My flaws now have light upon them,

no longer do they hide in immaturity.

Perhaps that means you would truly know me,

that we may build a stronger reality,

one which stands the assault of time.

Surgeon General Warning

My doctor asked when I would stop.

When do I plan on putting down the bottle.

When do I plan on snuffing out my smoke.

He tapped his pen against my chart,

peered through smudged spectacles.

His distant concern was almost believable,

but it was undermined by his glances at the clock.

I told him what I tell myself:

I drink to stir the demons.

They sit comfortably within my soul,

their new-found home.

Gin frustrates them,

floods their home,

causing them to stir.

They come alive,

clawing within me,

Making me write my verses.

I could write of happiness,

and other fleeting facades,

but I choose to embrace the pain.

Years have passed,

the pain has dulled,

Hidden deep in my scars.

Gin fills the scars,

flushing the memories out,

allowing me to write truth once more.

I smoke to calm the demons.

Once stirred they never leave,

the smoke chases them away,

pushes them back to their homes,

hiding them away,

until I need them again.

He stopped tapping,

told me my time was short,

said each drink removes a year,

each inhale removes two.

I told him I know,

but death comes no matter what,

my poetry will last forever,

I'll sacrifice years of my life,

if that's what it takes to write,

write something worth reading.

End

Is it remarkable, that I choose to write these lines?

Am I the first to question the cruelties of life?

Surely, I am just another scribe, in an unending chain.

Men and women throughout time,

bound together by their willingness to sift through the filth.

www.ingramcontent.com/pod-product-compliance
Lightning Source LLC
Chambersburg PA
CBHW020920090426
42736CB00008B/714